H. E. Wiseman

Judging from the Past and Present,

what are the prospects for good architecture in London? : A lecture

delivered in the theatre of the South Kensington Museum, on Tuesday the

12th of April, 1864

H. E. Wiseman

Judging from the Past and Present,
what are the prospects for good architecture in London? : A lecture delivered in the
theatre of the South Kensington Museum, on Tuesday the 12th of April, 1864

ISBN/EAN: 9783337426248

Printed in Europe, USA, Canada, Australia, Japan

Cover: Foto ©Suzi / pixelio.de

More available books at **www.hansebooks.com**

*Judging from the Past and Present, what are the
Prospects for Good Architecture in London?*

A LECTURE

DELIVERED IN THE

THEATRE OF THE SOUTH KENSINGTON MUSEUM,

ON TUESDAY THE 12TH OF APRIL, 1864.

By H. E. CARDINAL WISEMAN.

LONDON:

JOHN MURRAY, ALBEMARLE STREET.

1864.

LECTURE,

&c.   &c.

It is now many years since, early on a fine morning in the spring,—doubly so, in the spring of life and of the year,—that I found myself one of a party hastening along the road which leads from the Porta Capena to the Church of St. Sebastian, outside the walls of Rome. Others were before us, single, or in groups, and not a few were following us; so that when we reached our trysting-place, by the tomb of Cæcilia Metella, we formed a large gathering of youths, who soon clustered like bees round the learned Professor Nibby. For he was to be our leader and instructor in an antiquarian expedition; and he was now making his lucid preliminary address.

But it would not be incorrect to call this assembly our *meet*,—for we were going to open chase across the Roman Campagna, long before English hounds had coursed there. But it was not the fox nor the hare of which we were joining in pursuit,—we aimed at nobler quarry. It was for *cities* that we were going to hunt. Aye! for cities long lost, and only found again by our sagacious and intrepid guide a few years before, in 1824.

We first stumbled along over the ruins of the old Appian Way,—not then, as now, thanks to the care

of the reigning Pontiff, practicable, even in a carriage ; and having reached the supposed site of
Bovillæ, now Fratocchio, plunged into the outspread
plain of the Campagna ; and after visiting other
interesting ruins, reached the principal objects of
our search.

These were the sites of Apiolæ and Politorium.
If the discovery did not remunerate our toil over
the sultry plain, by any gratification of sense, it
repaid us at least by moral suggestions.

The walls of each city, if it deserved the name,
were clearly traceable. In one instance the enclosure
was divided by an interior wall into two divisions,
which prompted the application to this town of
the plural name, according to the analogy of other
ancient cities. A bridge (popularly, *il Ponte delle
Streghe*, the Witches' Bridge), leading to the gate
of one, remained entire ; its huge blocks of uncemented Alban stone (*peperino*) still holding fast
their places in the unbroken arch.* It has since
been destroyed.

You may naturally ask me what is the history
of these two cities, when were they built, by whom,
and wherefore destroyed ; and, consequently, how
long they have remained desolate.

Almost the only record that remains of their
annals is that of their destruction. Livy mentions
Apiolæ as having been conquered by Tarquinius
Priscus, and after a fresh rebellion destroyed and

---

* In Sir W. Gell's ' Map of Rome and its Environs' this bridge is given
to Mugilla, another of the cities alluded to in the text. But see Nibby,
quoted in the next note.

burnt by Ancus Martius; and Dionysius gives the
same account with more details. And Pliny speaks
of Politorium as one of the Latian cities, of which not
a trace remains.* For several other cities, between
Rome and Alba, shared the same fate. And in this
state of complete desolation they have remained,
unspoken of, and perhaps unseen, except by the
unheeding herdsman, for centuries. Of their sisters
not a trace has been found by the discoverer of these
two. Hence, perhaps, our little army of adventurous
archæologists was the largest that had passed the
gates of these primæval Latian cities since the days
of Rome's legendary monarchs.

The question very naturally presents itself to our
minds—What becomes of demolished cities? Here
and for miles round, there were no villages, no farm-
buildings, not any ruins of villas, formed possibly of
materials drawn from their remains; not even mounds
of grass-grown earth, that resembled the grave of a
departed town. Yet Livy tells us that the Roman
king gave splendid games to his subjects, with the
rich spoils which he carried home from one of these
cities. Does time grind down solid stone, and
scatter it, as dust, over the face of the earth; or
does this parent of the original materials of construction gradually reabsorb them into its maternal
bosom, when deprived of shape and place? Certain
it is, that here and elsewhere the work of destruction
may be so complete, that Nature reasserts her laws

---

* Livy, i. 25, 33. See Nibby, ' Analisi della Carta dei Contorni di
Roma.' Rome, 1837. Vol. i. p. 215 ; ii. p. 572.

and rights, and gradually, but surely, resumes her
sway over the usurpations of man.*

Yet man is not without the power to stamp his
footprints so heavily into his conquests, as that, if
won back by Nature, she cannot efface them, even
by the force of all her combined agencies,—the
earthquake, the storm, or the wearing action of ages.
On a coast as bare as the Campagna, stand the huge
and yet elegant temples of Pæstum, more imposing
by the solitude which surrounds them, fresh, com-
paratively, and young, while all else has perished.

And in Sicily there yet stand at Segeste, at
Salinuntum, and at Agrigentum, similar monuments
of man's genius, skill, and strength; columns erect,
unmoved, upon their platforms, or as at Salinuntum,
laid on the ground like soldiers slain in battle, still
keeping their ranks, after the earthquake which
overthrew, but could not destroy, the magnificent
work of remote ages.

If my preliminary observations brought us to the
conclusion that cities might so totally perish as not
to leave even a trace behind, we may be considered
I trust to have gained one more step by the instances
just mentioned—that the memory of a city is preserved by the survival only of great, solid, always
public, and always beautiful architectural works.

Two points seem here to deserve further elucida-
tion. . First, I have alluded to these posthumous

* It would be easy to multiply similar examples without going to the
East, where great and noble cities have totally disappeared. The ancient
Falernum, now Santa Maria di Falleri, is clearly traceable by its walls with
their gates, but the buildings have left no vestige behind them.

memorials as exclusively of one class; secondly, I have described them as beautiful.

I have, indeed, only mentioned the buildings of Pæstum and of Sicily, which are all *public* buildings, temples, theatres, walls, reservoirs, and tombs, for these last must be considered as having been under public guardianship. But further investigation will verify the validity of this statement.

What remains of Athens but its Erychtheum, its Temple of the Winds, its splendid Parthenon and other public edifices? Where are the houses of Pericles, or of Plato, or Demosthenes, or of any other of her worthies? Not a wall, however solidly built, has been left standing. And along that line of colossal monuments which is threaded by the Nile, temples, pyramids, and Memnoniums, with their carvings, and even their paintings, fresh without and within them, is there one single private building, from a cottage to a princely mansion, remaining; though, no doubt, hundreds and thousands of dwellings must have been built and rebuilt, to furnish workmen for these sumptuous edifices and princes to command their erection?

And so of Tadmor or Palmyra, and so of Balbek, and so of Persepolis, and so finally of Ellora, and the Indian cavern-temples, vast and solid—nay, sometimes elegant and slender, but always public—edifices are all that have outlived the destructive powers of man and of nature; and they appear so totally separated from the men, or even the race that constructed them, that we are tempted to adopt the prevailing superstition of the East, that not men, but Jins or Genii, raised them in the wilderness in waywardness or mockery.

But Rome will most effectually test the correctness of our principle. It is full of memorials of the past. Baths, hippodromes, amphitheatres, markets, exchanges, forums, aqueducts, gates, mausoleums, basilicas, prisons, the treasury, the Græcostasis, triumphal arches and columns are still standing, but more than all, temples of every form and dimension, round and quadrangular, vast and small. Sometimes these buildings are isolated, sometimes they stand in groups as they do in the Roman forum. They cover the seven hills, filling its vineyards and gardens. Yet of the dwellings of the inhabitants nothing beyond shapeless lumps here and there remains.

Descending thence to the Campus Martius, where the later city stood, we find the magnificent Pantheon almost intact. Its bronze ceilings have been stripped off within only a few centuries, but its noble portico, its huge bronze gates, its marble lining and its elegant columns stand in all their integrity and solemn beauty, while its precious pavement is unworn by the showers which, since the beginning of the Christian era, have poured down on it through its open, unglazed dome. Yet it is situated in the midst of a modern city, without a vestige, much less a fragment, of any coeval private building around it. More than ten generations of houses have probably succeeded one another, while it has remained unshaken.

What, I ask again, has become of the dwellings of contemporaries of these great works? The man who was rich enough to raise at his expense such a temple, and public Thermæ besides, did not build himself, depend upon it, a flimsy house. This was Agrippa; but neither did Crassus, nor Lucullus, nor Mæcenas, nor other wealthy and luxurious men in the days of solid construction and enduring materials. We know where the house and immense gardens of this last-named patron of art and letters were situated, and where were the houses of the Cornelii, of Sallustius, of Sylla, of Cicero, even those of Catulus, of Clodius, and of Scaurus; but of the buildings themselves we can find no remains.

Neither can it be said that the cause must be sought in the more perishable nature of the materials employed respectively in public and in private edifices. This is not so. On the contrary, many of the public buildings are constructed with uncemented blocks of *tufo,* friable and liable to flake. The private ones were built of calcareous stone, hard and durable, or of brick connected by the Roman mortar, made with *puzzolana,* to break which requires an operation more like that of quarrying or of mining than that of ordinary mason's work.

But that we may make ourselves still more sure of our principle, let us return again, in mind, to Sicily. In that island, so rich in early ruins, the most favoured spot is, without rivalry, Girgenti, the site of the ancient Agrigentum. It presents to the eye of the astonished artist and antiquarian piles almost of buildings, colossal in their proportions, massive in their uncemented blocks, columns, gigantic statues

(Persian captives) that supported walls, and enormous architraves. These were on such a scale in one instance that a man, we are told, could stand within one of the flutings of a pillar.

Yet this mass of buildings, to have erected which might seem beyond the resources, pecuniary and mechanical, of Paris or London, stands upon a desert plain; for the modern city, as if awe-struck by those giants below, has shrunk under the shelter of the ancient citadel. It is surrounded by no lesser ruins, no pigmy habitations.

Did the men who built the temples reserve for themselves none of their immense wealth, to enjoy in homes proportioned to the ideas exhibited in their public buildings? We cannot imagine it; and, indeed, it would be contrary to fact to suppose it. On the contrary, Agrigentum displayed a luxury not equalled in any modern capital. Its inhabitants lived sumptuously, and employed silver for their water-tanks. They prided themselves on the fleetness and beauty of their horses, and the brilliancy of their ivory equipages. When Exænetus, their fellow-citizen, had won a prize at the Olympian games, his chariot, upon entering into his native town, was followed, as Diodorus tells us, by three hundred others, each drawn by milk-white coursers.

That men of this character built themselves good houses we cannot doubt; but we have the strongest authority for the fact. Pindar calls it the fairest of cities. Empedocles, himself a citizen of Agrigentum, is said to have remarked, " that they built their houses as if they were to live for ever, but gave themselves up to luxury as if they were to die to-morrow." *

If from the contemplation of such greater monuments as have thus far occupied our attention, we turn to places and objects of secondary importance, we shall find the same results.

Wherever, for example, a town is celebrated for one signal remnant of antiquity, it is sure to be a public edifice. Thus Verona, Arles, Nismes, Taormina in Sicily, and Pola in Istria, have theatres; Nismes, moreover, its *maison carrée*; Ancona, the triumphal arch of Trajan ; Rimini and Fano (*Fanum Fortunæ*), their arches of Augustus ; Volterra, a gate; Cora and Assisi,† elegant porticoes; Tibur, its most graceful templet, crowning a richly-coloured rock ; while Palestrina, with its Roman palace and cathedral, is seated at ease on the terraces of Sylla's Temple of Fortune. It is everywhere the same ; only public buildings have hitherto defied time and its accidents; and form the monuments of buried cities and of their extinct races.

This has then become a law, so much the more general and certain, for its only exception. Fortunately for antiquarian science, but most unhappily for the poor inhabitants of Pompeii, their city was not left to the pining and wasting action of time; but

* Diog. Laert. viii. 2, § 63. See all the authorities on this subject, brought together in Dr. Smith's 'Dictionary of Greek and Roman Geography,' vol. i., *Agrigentum*.

† If I remember right, after more than twenty years, the vestibule at Assisi contains an inscription, advertisement, or epitaph, of one who is styled "medicus, chirurgus, oculista, dentista," evidently a general practitioner.

was struck down in the vigour and pride of health, to be
dissected at ease by the archæologue of the eighteenth
and subsequent centuries. Submerged in a deluge of
bland, insinuating ashes, which penetrated into the
most remote corners and crevices of every building;
embalmed, instead of being petrified like its twin city
Herculaneum, Pompeii has given us the only practical and sensible illustrations of what writers had let
us know about their domestic arrangements. The
peculiarity and singularity of this case only make
the otherwise universal rule absolute. It is this:

" That hitherto, in every country, and under all cir-
cumstances, the only edifices which have survived the
destruction of a city are public buildings; and that
our real acquaintance with the architecture of any
country in ancient times is derived exclusively from
these monuments." *

But I have to explain why I spoke in such general
terms of these edifices as *beautiful*.

The expression was deliberate, though it may
sound equivocal. When we have to select for the
future, we may have, and if we can we may indulge,
our preferences; in judging of the past we must ac-
cept its legacies, and value them by its standards.
If I wish to build a church, or a town-hall, or a
mansion, I may naturally select mediæval types.
But not on that account would I say that the Par-

---

* The same may be said of later monuments. There are villages in
which the church, still perfect, or partly ruined, towers over a few and poor
remnants of a former town, in strange and noble disproportion to its actual
occupants. Such, for example, are the old churches at Minster or Win-
chelsea in England, Damm in Flanders, Corbie in France, &c.

thenon is not most beautiful, and the monuments of Egypt most sublime.

In fact, considering architecture as a fine art, as the solid record of the power, genius, and thought of a people, we may say that when a nation or a race has reached the height of its civilization, according to its own self-created type, its indigenous, home-bred, time-matured culture, and then by its buildings gives expression to its principles and its feelings, with all the impressiveness which it commands, what it produces cannot fail to be beautiful in connection with these manifestations. In Egypt the feelings of servile awe and abject submission of a people towards a monarchy and a priesthood may be read in the wasteful magnificence of its pyramids, in the costly vanity of its obelisks, and in the gloomy mysticism of its temples. The elegance of mind and polished manners, eloquence and poetry of tongue in Greece, are all built up imperishably in Parian marble. The rude energy, perseverance, and the conqueror's power to make others' skill subserve its own deficiencies, which marked the Roman character from its kings to its Cæsars, manifest themselves from the massive blocks of its great drain, or the substructions of the Capitol, to the Corinthian columns of the Forum or the Pantheon.

And so, while the monuments of India, of Persia, of Assyria, of all the East, clearly represent a state of tyranny in peace and of savageness in war, the West, by its multiplied theatres, its palatial baths, its many basilicas or justice-halls, no less describes the condition of a relaxed, luxurious, and voluptuous

population, heedless of all serious cares, and willingly
leaving to any despot the trouble of enlarging the
boundaries of the empire, or of defending them
against barbarians, so long as to them were thence
supplied largesses without price, and the festival of a
triumph—*Panem et Circenses.*

And hence while Ramses may have loved to be
painted as holding in his hand, like puppet-strings,
the tresses of conquered sovereigns, to be beheaded
by the score with one stroke of his scimiter, or
crushed by one blow of his mace; and while the
kings of Nineveh had themselves sculptured with
grisly heads counted beside them after the battle-field,
the Roman emperor preferred to be seen on his
triumphal-car, bearing the golden spoils of the
Temple, while the ample wings of Victory crowning
him shut out from effeminate eyes the horrors of his
sack and of its carnage.

And thus the style of building, resulting from the
various experiences of growth in civilization, becomes
historical, apt, suggestive, and so beautiful. The
Northern slopes his roof to a lofty point, and then
crowns it with a spire, that it may shake off lustily
the superincumbent snow, or give easy flow to the
waters, and sharp resistance to the winds of an in-
clement climate. The Egyptian strengthened the
base of his edifice, and scientifically leaned its walls
inwards, for double security against earthquake or
inundation. For the danger lay at the foundations
and lower courses of his structure. And surely an
experience of two thousand years has shown that the
Greeks at home, and in their colonies, knew well

what they were about, however light or airy may
have been the architecture of their houses, when they
raised in the middle of their cities, and feared to
replace or to build aught else near in rivalry, those
huge baseless Doric columns on their massive plat-
form of rock or rocklike masonry, which have braved
every destructive effort of nature and of man. And
are *they* not thus doubly beautiful?

Even when not so artistically, are they not monu-
mentally? In this way Rome, by its eclectic style,
characterised most especially in the Villa of Adrian,
collective, imitative, but on reduced scales, shows
herself the mistress of the world in power, but its
disciple in the arts.

An additional clear deduction then from observa-
tion of the past is this, that wherever monuments
have been left us of architectural power and grandeur,
these qualities have been exhibited in a characteristic
style, according to national types, not varying from
age to age; still less from year to year. There was a
principle in architecture distinct from taste. The
second might change, but the first was invariable.
Along the valley of the Nile, from its mouth to
Philæ, there runs one order. The type of the
Pharaohs and that of the Ptolemies is but one. And
so from Athens to Sicily, with a long span of ages,
the Doric model binds together the Colonies with
their Grecian fatherland.

If our deductions from the past be just, first, that
in the public buildings must be laid the seeds of a
durable and imperishable architecture, and secondly,
that in these should be exhibited a consistent,

principled, national character of that Art, not an
ephemeral, variable, still less a capricious style of
building : having thus interrogated the *past*, and
heard its oracular answer, we must now look at the
present to arrive at our auguries about the *future*.
For such is our theme.

Have we then as yet gained this supreme and
vital point ? Have we any pretensions to an architectural system which all of us recognise as belonging
to our age and country, the child of its peculiar
civilization, the offspring of our climate and soil, and
of the special tastes inspired by our love of nature ?
Or have we forms and models that have sprung from
our institutions, our own domestic and insular pre-
dilections ?   In fact, looking at our great public
buildings of the day, will not a future age keep its
judgment equally balanced on the question, whether
we had decided between the classical style of the
Treasury, or the mediæval of the national palace, as
best recording our tastes and feeling ?

If this be so, must we not say, that looking at the
past which has given us rules, and at the present which
gives us data, our conclusion for the future of Architecture is not favourable, so far as public building is
concerned ?   Each edifice may be good—thoroughly
and even perfectly good of its kind—but together
they give no whole, no type, no system.   They will
bear witness to our skill and prosperity, not to our
consistency in Art.

It would be unfair to leave our subject here, and
not glance at the splendid efforts made by private
enterprise to redeem the architectural reputation of

our age. And I do so with pleasure, for two reasons : first, because they are indications of a new spirit which may become national ; secondly, because they are characteristic, so far, of our social condition.

There can be no doubt, therefore, that there is a manifest change in the desires for a better architecture, and those desires are gradually yet quickly giving themselves expression in action. We cannot walk the streets of London, especially those parts which are naturally the scenes of greatest activity, without being struck by the greater elevation, mass, and even elegance, which characterise not merely new buildings, but those which replace older and ruder edifices, known by a name which at once is antithetic to all ideas of beauty—warehouses. They have become streets of industrial palaces, contrasting most favourably with the rectilinear streets which still array, in stiff and cold monotony,' the dwellings of the rich.

Indeed it must be owned that the architectural movement of London is not among these. With a few exceptions of noble mansions newly built, we more frequently see, especially in a square, a house of ample dimensions, if not of elegant form, being mercilessly cut into two, or further subdivided, than anything fair and great springing up.

The many new streets in Westminster, and near Hyde Park and Kensington, present rows of splendid looking houses, which may be well characterised as *imposing*, for they receive much of their outward grandeur from their stucco clothing ; nor is there either the solidity of construction, or the character

C

of style, which can lead to the formation of a national Art.

If from these centres of more impressive edifices we wander to the suburbs, we find the same endless lines of sameness; so identical that house after house might seem to have been shaped under the same mould, carried on from site to site; and to be inscribed, each in one line of the contractor's book, with a simple *Do.* opposite the same repeated figures.

It is then to the commercial element of our social condition that we have to look for the growing prospects of London architecture; leaving those whose resources are in their country ancestral estates, to build on their property, as they do often very splendidly.

On this account I said just now, with satisfaction, that the improvements in this branch of Art are characteristic of our national condition. For it is the period of immense commercial prosperity, successful enterprise, and almost fabulous wealth; and it is right that this varied result of national industry should be read on its edifices so long as they may last.

The principle of such a connection may indeed be found in an older combination gradually increased. For any one standing at a point where he could see the Bank, the Exchange, the Mansion House, the Goldsmiths' Hall, and the Telegraph Office, would feel that his eye grasped the very keys of England's financial greatness, each wrought in forms not inharmonious, and superior to what any other standpoint in the metropolis presents.

And so it is but natural to expect that the union of the same two principles will act similarly in the neighbourhood of such examples, and that an improved taste will be ministered to, and even brought to life, by increased means of indulging it.

Still though we may give just praise to the efforts of the present, let us not forget that our looks are toward the future. And what we have to do is—augur from the one to the other.

It is certain that in former periods and in other countries the commercial power, when at its height, moulded the architecture of cities into a consistent and enduring type, sometimes picturesque, at other times grand. Take Bruges, Antwerp, Cologne, Nürnberg, and in part Amsterdam, as instances of the first.* The gable, with its many stories, turned to the street, for mercantile purposes, gave a principle harmonious with the greater architecture of church-buildings, with its pointed front : turrets and elegant niches, with images at every "coign of vantage," windows whose lanceolated tracery repeated gracefully the great outlines of the structure ; such were the features which those old merchant-cities, in different degrees, still present. But here our

---

* Far beyond the range of cities mentioned in the text, in Germany and France, extends this picturesque architecture, not merely because a type once created is naturally adopted, beyond the place of its origin, but also because it was found, no doubt, well suited for domestic economy. The French word *grenier*, originally the grange, or granary, now means an attic; because the provision of grain, and other stores, were first, and for once, carried to the dry top of the strong, well-built house, whence the domestics had the lighter toil of bringing them *down* in detail. Was not this a wise economy? Now we send our coals, for instance, a story *lower* than the ground, to have them carried up to a third or fourth floor above it. But then we do not build for the older arrangement.

principle returns : while the grand old minster, and
the lofty city-hall, with its quaint chimes, still stand
storm and time-proof, the characteristic dwellings of
those who built them are gradually declining from
their type, are being taken down and replaced by
modern square blocks, more and more slender at
every remove; till, at length, the old experience may
be confirmed, that even without any disaster occur-
ring, public edifices alone are lasting and monumental.*

Of the grand, as characteristic of a national architecture, equally embracing public and private construction, we may consider Venice as an illustration.
One style pervades the city of merchant princes,
formed during the days when her argosies never
returned from a voyage without a column for the
walls, or a gem for the shrines, of San Marco.

But, on the other hand, are the clearly expressed
wishes for a better architecture in London such as
to promise an enduring and acknowledged principle
of it in future ?   In fact not yet; in tendency very
probably.

With the class of modern buildings which I have
spoken of, it is both just and necessary to couple
another.   I allude to the numerous churches, schools
and other institutions of charity, which have risen
in every part of the capital, and which, though of
their nature they may be said to be public buildings,

---

* In Nürnberg, I believe, there is a municipal regulation which obliges
all houses to be rebuilt upon the ancient model.   It is undoubtedly the most
picturesque, and most representative of ancient, among modern cities.

yet are erected chiefly by private benevolence, directed by private taste.

Returning for a moment to the more secular edifices of which I have spoken, I invite you once more to pass before them. You will find, indeed, much to admire, and to make you feel that England possesses many architects equal to any undertaking, and possessing great individual abilities and taste. But over their works no harmonizing principle seems to rule. Here you have a Norman, and beside it a Pointed building; in this the Byzantine, in the next the Venetian; in its neighbour the Renaissance prevails, through a miscellaneous combination. Some run into that style, which is steadily gaining ground, in the second class of semi-public buildings.

It is in these that we find general taste gravitating towards somewhat, which may be the germ of a national Art; though I must be pardoned if I express a hope that in its growth it may be purged and stripped of what as yet is rude and unwieldy.

In the large piles of building for religious, or charitable purposes, there seems to be a preference for mass, relieved only by strongly contrasting colours, often grimly disposed, unsuggestive, not seldom too horizontally directed. Symmetry,* which after all,

---

* Is there not an inclination to consider symmetry in the exterior of a building as a sacrifice of principle to appearance? We are told that the elevation should follow the ground-plan, and be carried up, guided by it, without attempting exteriorly symmetrical dispositions. Surely such a principle argues imperfection in art, by going in direct opposition to great principles in nature.

Though great mineral masses are unsymmetrical, crystallography shows the tendency, even in the lowest order of creation, to assume a symmetrical arrangement of particles. In plants this is more apparent. Not only

does deserve some respect, seems to be sometimes studiously despised; prominences and relief, so necessary for chiaro-oscuro and artistic effects, are rigorously excluded; while immense plates of wall, mostly of brick, the poorest of materials, rise to a dizzy height above all surrounding buildings.

This rough and ready style of building is carried into the interior of even the most sacred edifices. Were our brickwork like that employed in the buildings of Nero's time, almost close-fitting as carved stone, without visible cement, uniform in shape and tender in colour, sharply moulded into every architectural member and ornament, and put into every comely disposition that can copy, without simulating, stone, one would be glad to see such an adaptation of a material, cheap, manageable, and everywhere at hand.

But I must own that as it is now sometimes em-

---

flowers are essentially *homologous*, side corresponding with side, but the entire tree seems to possess an instinct for symmetry : if pyramidal, throwing out its shoots equally all round, or otherwise giving roundness and equal mass to all parts of its head.

But it is in animals, and especially in His noblest work, that the Great Architect manifests a power which in man we might call ingenuity, in Him simple wisdom, of making the visible portion of His work perfectly symmetrical, while the interior of His structure is (with the exception of the head) completely devoid of that quality. Beginning with the heart, neither each organ in itself, nor the position of one to the other, bears any trace of symmetrical arrangement. This is the perfection of the rule, that the inward structure may be admirably complete without any symmetry, and with individual reference of each part to its own action and end ; while outwardly that symmetry may be preserved without sacrifice of plan, but in natural harmony with those senses, which the head is built symmetrically, within as without, expressly to supply in accordance with that principle of external symmetry.

Must not the most perfect of man's architectural works be that which assumes and acts upon this model of creative wisdom ?

ployed, it does not appear to be in its place ; nor do
I think it necessary to say why.

But in the place where I am now addressing you,
justice, as well as an agreeable inclination, invites me
to mention, with willing and hopeful praise, a new
material, now successfully applied in the new buildings of the Kensington Museum, and promising to
take an important place in our future architectural
works. This is *terra-cotta*, or baked earth ; which,
formed by an artist with any amount of genius and
taste, is hardened by the artificer up to the dura-
bility of ancient pottery, and serves at once to make
a solid building, and its imperishable ornaments.
And, one is sorry to be obliged always to add as a
recommendation, it is not expensive.

However, without implying blame, where I have
neither the skill, nor the right to judge, and assuming
that a certain necessity here, as elsewhere, compels
the artist to make the best of the worst materials,
. I will repeat, that in these various attempts we see
the feeling by the feet for a better path, and the
stretching of the hands for a higher grasp. By
degrees, genius will strike, out of what is merely
tentative, something novel and permanent ; the tem-
porary larva will drop off, and the graceful and
elegant remain, and prosper.

If a new architecture thus arises, and takes its
place among the arts of ages, it will soon have its
Leone Albertis, its Palladios, its Vignolas ; who will
give its rules, and true proportions, and show it
perhaps to be rhythmical and harmonic, as are the
depressed tympanums of the old Doric, and the high-

peaked fronts of our ancient cathedrals.* Architects will then be no longer tempted to startle and amaze by astounding novelties, but will seek to please by harmonies that give the eye repose. And it will be felt that the architect is not a builder up only, but a beautifier, of his materials, of their arrangement, and of their uses.

But, in thus strongly advocating an architecture not depending on private exertions, or individual taste, but possessed of stable maxims and a national character, am I contemplating the possibility of this mighty city being the victim of some frightful catastrophe, which may destroy, or devastate it, and leave but solitary pillars, or broken arches, on a huge plain, to mark the spot where throbbing millions once discoursed and did many good and great things?

Not by any means. Our times are too homely for the enormities of former days. When conflagrations consumed the great cities of antiquity, there was no fire-engine in every parish; the earthquake is a stranger to our unvolcanic soil, though it paid us a passing visit lately; and diplomacy has taken the place of ploughing up cities, and sowing them with salt.†

But in our eventful days, and with our energetic population, we have other possible changes before us. We are building on a shifting soil. The ancient city of Volterra is subject to periodical landslips, known by the peculiar name of *balzi*. It is situated near the edge of a crumbling hill, at the foot of which

---

* See Lecture ' On the Points of Contact between Science and Art,' p. 65.
† As in the destruction of the Belgian and Ionian forts.

runs a gnawing stream. In spite of most costly pre-
cautions, ever and anon, the earth yields, and down
rushes an avalanche of buildings, fortunately cleared
of their forewarned inhabitants. When I was there,
some years ago, a church and convent were, apparently and literally, on the brink of destruction. It
reminded one of ancient fables, where the natives of
a country have periodically to propitiate a marine
monster, by some precious human offering.

And so, in some sort, it is with us. We have
no security that the commerce of the· City may not
decline one day, or migrate; and what becomes of
the lines of handsome store-houses which now occupy
entire streets? Other uses must be found for them,
probably less remunerative; or they may be left
untenanted. In either case, a change will come over
them : they may share eventually the fate of Tyre
and Syracuse.

This, however, may be, and I trust will be, a very
remote,. or even an impossible event. But in another way, London is ever changing its condition,
and needing reparation. It appears to me sometimes like one of those immense overgrown shrubs
in a garden, which, after some years, begins to die
out in the middle, and leaves there a painful hollow.
There are many streets, once inhabited by wealthy
families, now gradually devoted to offices for busi-
ness. There are many others in the centre of
London, which the daily increase of legal demands
is converting from abodes to chambers.

And, when the learned profession of the law
throws its meshes over any district, architecturally

it decidedly exercises a deteriorating influence. In
its public capacity it is great and noble; as the new
library and hall, in Lincoln's Inn, well prove. But
I am speaking of the private abodes of jurisprudence,
as they take possession of a new neighbourhood.
The houses become dingier; there is a cobwebby
appearance about areas and lobbies; and did we not
know that our friends within can and do keep their
hands cleaner than they do their windows, they
would be approached with more of reverential awe,
and less of sincere affection than are now their meed.

In time these gaps made in the very heart of the
metropolis must be made up; and we cannot afford
to restore the same old forms of what Canova is
said to have called "long brick walls, with rows of
slits in them." There is not a more melancholy
exemplification of decayed grandeur than a London
street which has once been "respectable," and keeps
up, in its desolation, the same unvarying forms as
some neighbouring thoroughfare, at whose doors the
carriage still lingers. One after another these parts
of the city must fall into decay,—for they have been
built on calculation of that end,—and it is vain,
though painful, to conjecture what will be their next
phase.

Thus baffled in our attempts to penetrate the
future, let us rest in the present, to seek further
light from it and from the past. We are obliged to
confess, on comparing these two periods, that there
is wanting in our times a quality anciently remark-
able, and of great importance to the furtherance of
good architecture in the future.

After consideration, I do not think I shall be wrong in calling it *reverence*. I mean by it, that respect for what is good, or sacred, or historical, or beautiful in itself, or in its associations, which will consider these attributes worthy of being balanced against momentary convenience or material gain. There is certainly a character of brute force in the disposition to knock down every thing that stands in your way ; while there is a graceful ingenuity, and a power of genius, manifested in attaining your aim without violating respected feelings. A man of taste, while he traces a path through his ancestral woods, avoids felling some trees, whether distinguished for their beauty or hallowed by some family reminiscence.

Now the lowest scale on which this want of reverence is shown, is in the total disregard for our Art itself. I fear our people are not as yet well educated respecting it. They know that a picture or a statue is "a work of art ; " they hardly know that a building may be, and ought to be, equally so. They can estimate, no doubt, greatness in size and .height, but the graces and delicacies, the beauties of relative proportions, and the elegance of ornamentation, they do not yet appreciate. It would hardly be too much to say that many persons, if brought to the spot in the city which I have just now described, for the purpose of maturing some gigantic enterprise of a profitable character, would not take into consideration the artistic value of the buildings before them, or on that account decide they should be spared. They would weigh only their market price, and compute whether the intended

scheme would be profitable enough to buy up the
property required, and its management sufficiently
influential to carry the necessary legislative measures
for the purpose. In other words "money value" is
the principal, if not the only, estimate for land or
house, and many are indifferent whether the site is
occupied by a marble portico or by an iron and glass
dome.

It is sadly discouraging for an artist of sound and
feeling taste to think that he is building on a perishable foundation, on a moving sand ; that in a few
years his edifice may be wanted, in virtue of an irre-
sistible decree, and for a highly remunerative "consideration," as it is called, for some totally different
purpose, and must be misapplied, or perhaps even
removed ; that its beautiful and studied proportions
will be reduced to classified heaps of rubbish, beginning with "Lot No. 1," and going on in an indefinite
series, including cornices and architraves, elaborately
carved, in keeping with the whole design. Few
men, conscious of the dignity of their art, can labour
with any heart for so precarious and so ignoble a
futurity.

But there is a reverence for higher objects than
even Art. There is a natural reverence for whatever
is monumental or historical; and this feeling grows
and ripens to religious reverence. Neither of these
feelings seems to be much cultivated amongst us.
Take the following evidence from the "City Engineer's Report on Public Companies applying for Bills
in the present Session of Parliament."

"The Monument at Fish Street Hill, and Temple

Bar, Draper's Gardens, Finsbury Circus, Apothe-
caries' Hall, and portions of the *Times* Office are
scheduled, as are various of the City Halls and the
Admiralty at Whitehall." And again, " Public parks
and gardens are to be cut or tunnelled through." *

These extracts sufficiently justify us in saying that
there is a reckless disregard of public and monumental property in the exactions of projects for material changes, on this vexed soil of ours, into something
new and strange.

As to more religious objects, my own experience
may warrant somewhat. I have myself received this
year seven or eight notices of the intended destruction of churches, schools, orphanages, and other charitable institutions, to be ruthlessly demolished or
treacherously burrowed under. And my portion in
the danger must be but a small item in the general
fate.

Among the ancients, next to temples came the
burial-places of their ancestors, in claim to reverence.
Little indeed should we know of the Etruscans but
for the sacredness of their tombs. Immense riches
were buried in them, and wars, rebellions, tumults,
and cupidity equally respected these treasuries of
death. Gold and jewels, bronze furniture, not to
speak of paintings representing their games, their
feasts, and their domestic life, have been thence
brought to light, and store large museums.

Yet now the graves of ages are violated without
scruple, and I have heard with horror that the

* Mr. Haywood's Report, p. 65.

churchyard of old St. Pancras's, in which some of
my nearest of kin have reposed for more than half a
century, is given up for railway accommodation.

It may be said, And if we interrogate the past,
shall we not discover that the exigencies of an
increasing population exacted similar sacrifices of
reverential feeling? I answer, No. That feeling
would have over-ridden every other consideration.
Immense was the growth of population at the
Augustan period in Rome. But the streets of tombs,
which began outside every gate, were never allowed
to be touched; the Appian Way continues to pre-
serve even at the present day the resting-places of
the Scipios and Metelli. We have lost all record
of their homes, the latest posterity retains that of
their tombs. Even the Columbaria of the Freedmen,
or servants, of Augustus remain inviolate.

But such a new and startling evidence of this
reverence for what is monumental or sacred, in those
times, has lately come to light, that you must pardon
me, if I here introduce it as an illustration of my
subject. The imperial house or palace was begun
by Augustus, who preserved the simplicity of re-
publican habits, as a modest mansion, on the Palatine
hill of Rome. Each successive emperor added to it,
till Nero, not finding one hill sufficient to satisfy the
cravings of his extravagance, burnt down the dwellings on two neighbouring hills, and raised on their
ruins his Golden House.

The Palatine is now divided between three principal proprietors—the English College, which owns
the Circus Maximus; the nuns of the Visitation;

and the French Emperor. The last of these has bought the Orti Farnesiani, or Farnesian Gardens, from the King of Naples, and has thus become owner of the site of the imperial house.

His first care was to order a systematic and complete clearing of the ground—the first excavation ever made for purely architectural purposes. He committed the direction and execution of it to the Cavaliere Rosa, and he could not well have placed it in better hands.

The work commenced in 1861, and in the following year "a preliminary sketch" was given of the discoveries till then made, in the Roman Archæological Magazine,* by G. Henzen. Even then, the results were most interesting, though chiefly topographical. The division of the hill into two knolls (called Gemulus and Velia) and the two approaches to the palace, were soon discovered. By degrees the accumulated soil and rubbish have been removed; and the entire plan of the imperial abode has been laid bare. You walk on the precious pavements of its courts and halls, amidst the columns of its peristyles.

The palace is thus shown to have been a mere Roman house on a gigantic scale. The Atrium, or great entrance court, surrounded by pillars, is 3016 square metres, or 32,461 square feet in area; and the Tablinum, or inner court, 1408 square metres, or 15,156 square feet. The halls for imperial festivals are of a corresponding magnitude. The houses of Tiberius and of Caligula, that is the additions made by them to the palace, are easily discernible.

* 'Bullettino dell' Istituto Archeologico,' 1862, p. 225.

But it is not this magnificence that bears upon our subject, but what I am going to state. It so happened that when these emperors selected the Palatine for the site of their sumptuous buildings, they found it already occupied by several ancient monuments, sacred and profane. The principal ones were the *Supercilium Scalarum Caci*; the *Tugurium*, or cottage of Faustulus, Romulus's foster-father; the grove on the plain of Apollo's temple; the *Auguratorium*, or place of meeting for the augurs; and principally the temple of *Jupiter Propugnator*, built three hundred years before by Decius, after the Samnite war. We must perhaps add a Basilica, or Justice Hall, mentioned in the Acts of ancient Martyrs, and yet distinguishable in all its parts.

What was to be done with all these buildings existing inconveniently together on the site selected for the residence of the Cæsars? The answer seems obvious to our way of looking at such things. *We* should at once apply for an Act of Parliament, and have them thrown down or removed to other situations. Now surely the will of such men as those was stronger than any modern legislative enactment. Our prime ministers do not exactly dare to knock off the heads of all the opposition, or to order the mover and seconder of an adverse resolution to walk off to a Turkish bath, and have a vein opened, so to bleed luxuriously to death. A word, and down would go all the ancient and venerable monuments of kings and consuls.

But that word apparently durst not be spoken. As the Cavalier Rosa writes to me, even those cruel autocrats respected the public opinion, which by revering, saved those precious memorials. All of them and others were built in or round—simply, were embodied in the imperial residence.

In fact it was more than this. Tiberius, one of the most unsparing and self-willed of those despots, when he came to make his addition to the palace, found the temple of Jupiter, with its rude construction of Alban stone, right in his way. He did not remove it or mutilate it, but he built on a line divergent from that of his plan, so as to go behind it.

To such an extent did the feeling of reverence prevail, that it imposed laws not on subjects only, but on rulers. It curbed the will of obdurate tyrants, and forced from them deference to a power stronger than their own.

There can be no doubt that had those rulers of the universe defied public feeling, and overthrown the rude constructions of earlier Rome and the age-worn monuments of its kings, it would have been only to replace them by statelier and fairer structures. Such unfortunately is not the case in our demolitions. The railway projector does not contemplate the enrichment or embellishment of our city. He may destroy much that is not worth being preserved for its beauty, but it is generally to leave in its place something more unsightly; and if he does demolish what is worth preserving, it enters not into his plans to substitute anything better.

You will all have heard of the extent, reported by the City engineer, to which new railway schemes carry their competing designs, in that venerable por-

tion of our metropolis. It may be summed up in one
sentence. They require "about 160 acres only,
which is about *one-fourth* of the entire city ;" the
total length of railways proposed is about 20 miles ;
and "the various public ways of all descriptions
which are interfered with are about 300." *

The requirement of one-fourth of the area of a city
for the conveyance of the inhabitants of the remaining three-fourths, does indeed seem disproportioned.
But I am not disposed nor entitled to discuss this
great statistical point. The question is, could not
the ravages which necessity imposes be repaired,
and more deference be paid to that natural *piety*,
under which the ancients classed reverence for re-
ligion and respect for the departed ?

In contemplating the course of a railway through a
populous district, I am sometimes reminded of an
anecdote related to me by a gentleman who for
many years lived in Southern Africa. He occupied
a long low tenement—a bungalow—consisting of one
only room, which served him for every purpose, and
was situated in a wild district. One day as he was
writing at a table at one end of his apartment, he
heard a frightful crash at the other, and turning
round was aghast at what he beheld. A huge black
elephant, of the most formidable kind, had, it would
seem, been roaming in quest of some choice food for
his meal, when he met this Englishman's cottage in
his way. Being totally heedless of its value to any
one, he did not take the trouble to prefer his line
of deviation, and go round it, but walked straight

---

* Haywood, p. 64.

through it, undisturbed by the shower of roof and wall material which fell over his pachydermatous back. He coolly walked to the opposite wall—if he could be said to walk in a space scarcely longer than himself—set his fore-foot against it, and made himself a breach clean through it, which afforded him an exit as capacious as his entrance.

Just so does a new line come crashing and smashing through a lath-and-plaster region of the City, breaking down one end of a house, and passing, through the opposite side, into the next. But what is worse, the black elephant remains for ever, as if entranced, across the thoroughfare; solidly built upon an Act of Parliament, in the form of an iron tubular disfigurement. How can this new accident of our architectural condition be dealt with? Perhaps the past may be able to teach us.

There is nothing, at any previous period, which so nearly resembles the inroads of the railway into London, as the invasion, by aqueducts, of ancient Rome.

No one, who has visited that city, can have overlooked, or forgotten, those long lines of arches, sometimes unbroken for miles, which bestride the Campagna, like files of camels crossing the desert, and bringing to some isolated city the merchandise or the luxuries of a more favoured climate. And so, in sooth, they do. They are caravans, that hourly bring from the hill districts around, that most necessary quickener of languid life, and restorer of feverish existence, in a southern climate—delicious water in streams, sparkling and bounding over the arid sultriness of the way, and arriving fresh as if just struck out of the rock.*

To form some idea of the aqueducts of ancient Rome, we must glance at the present supply of water in that city, as the only term of comparison.

The ancient aqueducts were all 'cut off, in the sixth century, by Vitiges, king of the Goths, when he besieged Rome, defended successfully by Belisarius. No attempt was made to restore them, and for eleven centuries the inhabitants were compelled to drink no waters but those of the Tiber, and of cisterns.

The water of the Tiber easily and quickly parts with its deposit, and becomes clear and potable. Still, for the poor, it must have been a hardship to have to carry it home. But the ingenuity of charity sought to lighten this labour. A pious confraternity was formed, which had its seat at the Lateran Church, under the name of Aquarii, or "watermen," and devoted itself to supplying the poor with water.

So soon as the Roman Pontiffs had leisure to turn their minds to internal improvements, after their return from Avignon in 1377, one of their first thoughts was to recover some of the lost sources, and reconduct their waters to Rome. In the course of seventy years, three of them were again pouring out their grateful supplies into reservoirs, whence they are distributed through every part of the city, and flow on all sides—sometimes in torrents—into the most magnificent, or graceful, fountains.

To present to you a tangible way of measuring the quantity of water which these three aqueducts

* So symbolized on "the fountain of Moses," on the Quirinal.

bring into the city, I will give you the calculation made in 1857 by Signor Cavalieri di San Bertolo, long engineer to the water supply of Rome.*

Any one who has visited the Eternal City must have seen the great market-place, called Piazza Navona, on one side of which, occupying one-half of it, stand the great Pamphily palace, and the elegant church of St. Agnes. Now suppose that immense area to be enclosed, so as to become a reservoir, the walls of which shall rise to the roof of the palace; that reservoir would exactly contain the quantity of water that enters Rome every twenty-four hours.

Or, to reduce this fact to figures, it will be as follows, omitting fractions.

The area of the Piazza made quadrangular is 813 English feet by 170, or 66,586 square feet, which, raised to the height of about 66 feet, the elevation of the Palace, gives 4,282,507 cubic feet, or, if filled with water, 2,224,274 gallons of water.

This is the daily supply of modern Rome, brought by three aqueducts. It is at the rate of 321 gallons per day for every inhabitant.†

Now, keep in mind that this is the water furnished by *three* aqueducts; whereas ancient Rome was supplied by nineteen or twenty. There exists a Roman author (Frontinus) who has given us an account of their supplies, in measures tolerably explicable. The result is, that calculating the number of in-

---

* 'Sulle acque della moderna Roma,' Rome, 1859. The essay was read in the *Accademia Tiberina* in 1857.

† See the calculations in Cavalieri, p. 30. The population is put by the author at 175,214.

habitants in Rome, at the extravagant figure of
20,000,000, each person had for his share 172 gallons
of water.*

As the Romans always brought their waters along
a uniform level, what must have been the march of
these twenty aqueducts, not only across the plain,
but through the city, where we still trace them, in
the valleys between the hills?

The aqueducts are beautiful objects while stalking
across the country in their naked simplicity; and so
does the viaduct of a railway connecting two hills
often become a graceful addition to the landscape.
But in passing, or cutting, through the midst of a
city, it is very different. Can any one imagine that
the aqueducts of Imperial Rome strode along as they
did outside the wall, without a marble clothing, where
they emerged into the public sight, or that they
traversed the Forum, or climbed the Capitol, or
Palatine, in their inornate suit of grey *peperino?*

It is incredible.   Indeed, the number of bassi-
rilievi allusive to the flow of these waters, and
collected by Fabretti, which adorned the aqueducts
while yet outside the gates, as well as what we know
of the magnificence of Imperial Rome, forbids us to
imagine it possible.

But we have yet surviving evidence to the contrary. Twice in the course of their journey five
aqueducts meet at two gates of Rome, Porta Mag-
giore and Porta San Lorenzo, and have to cross one

* Cavalieri, p. 30. In Paris each inhabitant has only fifty litres or quarts
per day. Fabretti, in his classical work 'De Aquis et Aqueductis Veteris
Romae,' 1680, gives the catalogues of the 19 and 20 waters, p. 148.

over the other above the cornices of the gateways. This is strictly analogous to their crossing a street. Their channels are kept separate, so that the five water-courses rise considerably more than 20 feet above the crown of the gateway arch. If we confine ourselves to the gate of San Lorenzo, we find that the lowest begins immediately above this, occupying the cornice; the second is behind the pediment; and the three superior ones are masked by a lofty marble superstructure, or attic, covered with inscriptions of several emperors, giving most important information on the subject of the Roman waters.* Indeed, according to Fabretti, some antiquarians have maintained that the triumphal arch of Drusus, erected by Augustus, is in reality a disguise for an aqueduct passing over.

In the same way, no doubt, Roman emperors would have treated railways as they did aqueducts, had they existed, and *must* have penetrated into the heart of their city. They would have compelled them, whenever they came out into public view, to harmonise with the architecture which they were promoting, contribute to the embellishment of Rome, in their estimation the most beautiful of human creations—

"Rerum pulcherrima Roma,"

and to become even monumental.

Why should not this be done in London, more wealthy far than was the Rome of the Cæsars? I believe that an iron viaduct is to cross, if it has not

---

* An excellent view and section of this gateway is given in a discourse by Mgr. Borgnano, ' Dell' acqua di Q. Marcio Rè.' Rome, 1861.

done so, Ludgate Hill, in front of St. Paul's. It has
been denounced as an eyesore. But would not this
imputation be removed, if either side, besides architectural supports in fine proportions, bore, in that
very metal now become an artistic material, a relief,
which would not require high finish on account of its
scale and elevation, suited to the surface and to the
place? For example, not to wound religious suscep-
tibilities, the funeral processions of two men, among
our last heroes, whose biers passed beneath that spot,
might be represented, and record at once our military
and naval glories, in the honours awarded and paid
to Nelson and to Wellington.

The Company which has been so bitterly assailed
would gain immortal honour, and become a national
benefactor by an outlay that would hardly be greater
than that of a dozen girders.

I must conclude this very imperfect Lecture, so
kindly and patiently listened to. Glad indeed shall
I feel, if any sentiment which I have uttered should
prove fertile, ripening in better heads, and being
reaped by stronger hands. And happy shall I be if
even any new fact which I have produced should
assist, in any way, the efforts now made to advance
the progress of Art.

If I have spoken freely of defects, and still more of
dangers, I have done so in the desire of associating
better the resources of the engineer with those of the
artist. The impelling force of the one is necessity,
the attractive power of the other is grace. If the
first is compelled sometimes to produce practical

hideousness, why should not the latter drape it with even an elegant inutility? In a former Lecture I endeavoured to show how Science might bear Art on his stout shoulders when obliged to descend to the more practical things of earth; in this I have tried to suggest how Art may, in her turn, bear Science on her pinions, when he must fly across chasms, rise above mere mechanical performances, and boldly court the eye of an educated and now artistic people. Even if Science must emerge from its Cyclopean forges and its potent laboratories in the shape of a gigantic chimney, why should not Art fly up to it, and bestow on it elegance of proportions and some richness of details?

And so I close my Address to you, by expressing a sincere conviction that the prospects of Architecture are most promising, but that they will greatly increase in proportion as we can promote among all classes reverence for the sacred, and taste for the beautiful.

LONDON : PRINTED BY WILLIAM CLOWES AND SONS, STAMFORD STREET, AND CHARING CROSS.

www.ingramcontent.com/pod-product-compliance
Lightning Source LLC
Chambersburg PA
CBHW021600270326
41931CB00009B/1318